Dear Parent:
Your child's lov...

Every child learns to read in a different way and at his or her own speed. Some go back and forth between reading levels and read favourite books again and again. Others read through each level in order. You can help your young reader improve and become more confident by encouraging his or her own interests and abilities. From books your child reads with you to the first books he or she reads alone, there are I Can Read Books for every stage of reading:

SHARED READING
Basic language, word repetition, and whimsical illustrations, ideal for sharing with your emergent reader

BEGINNING READING
Short sentences, familiar words, and simple concepts for children eager to read on their own

READING WITH HELP
Engaging stories, longer sentences, and language play for developing readers

READING ALONE
Complex plots, challenging vocabulary, and high-interest topics for the independent reader

I Can Read Books have introduced children to the joy of reading since 1957. Featuring award-winning authors and illustrators and a fabulous cast of beloved characters, I Can Read Books set the standard for beginning readers.

A lifetime of discovery begins with the magical words **"I Can Read!"**

Visit www.icanread.ca for information
on enriching your child's reading experience.

I Can Read Book® is a trademark of HarperCollins Publishers

Ruth Graves Wakefield: One Smart Cookie
Text copyright © 2019 by HarperCollins Publishers Ltd.
Pictures © 2019 by Nick Craine.
All rights reserved. Published by Collins, an imprint of HarperCollins Publishers Ltd.

This work is adapted from a story of the same title in *5-Minute Stories for Fearless Girls* by Sarah Howden, illustrations by Nick Craine.

No part of this book may be used or reproduced in any manner whatsoever without the prior written permission of the publisher, except in the case of brief quotations embodied in reviews.

HarperCollins books may be purchased for educational, business, or sales promotional use through our Special Markets Department.

HarperCollins Publishers Ltd
Bay Adelaide Centre, East Tower
22 Adelaide Street West, 41st Floor
Toronto, Ontario, Canada
M5H 4E3

www.harpercollins.ca

Library and Archives Canada Cataloguing in Publication information is available upon request.

www.icanread.ca

ISBN 978-1-4434-5986-0

WZL 1 2 3 4 5 6 7 8 9 10

RUTH GRAVES WAKEFIELD:
ONE SMART COOKIE

by Sarah Howden
pictures by Nick Craine

Collins

Ruth Wakefield loved to cook.

And she was very good at it.

Ruth and her husband owned
a hotel called the Toll House Inn.
Ruth cooked all the food for
the hotel restaurant.

Ruth cooked buttery lobster dinners. She cooked tasty baked beans and meat loaf and roast chicken.

Everything Ruth made was good.
But she was best known for
her desserts.

Ruth made fudgy chocolate cakes.

She made gooey apple pies.

And Ruth made spicy gingerbread.

"This is the best food I've ever had," diners would say. "Then my work here is done," Ruth would say with a laugh.

Ruth was a very smart woman. She was always trying to make her cooking even better.

"Cooking is a science," Ruth would tell her husband, Kenneth. "I have to keep experimenting."

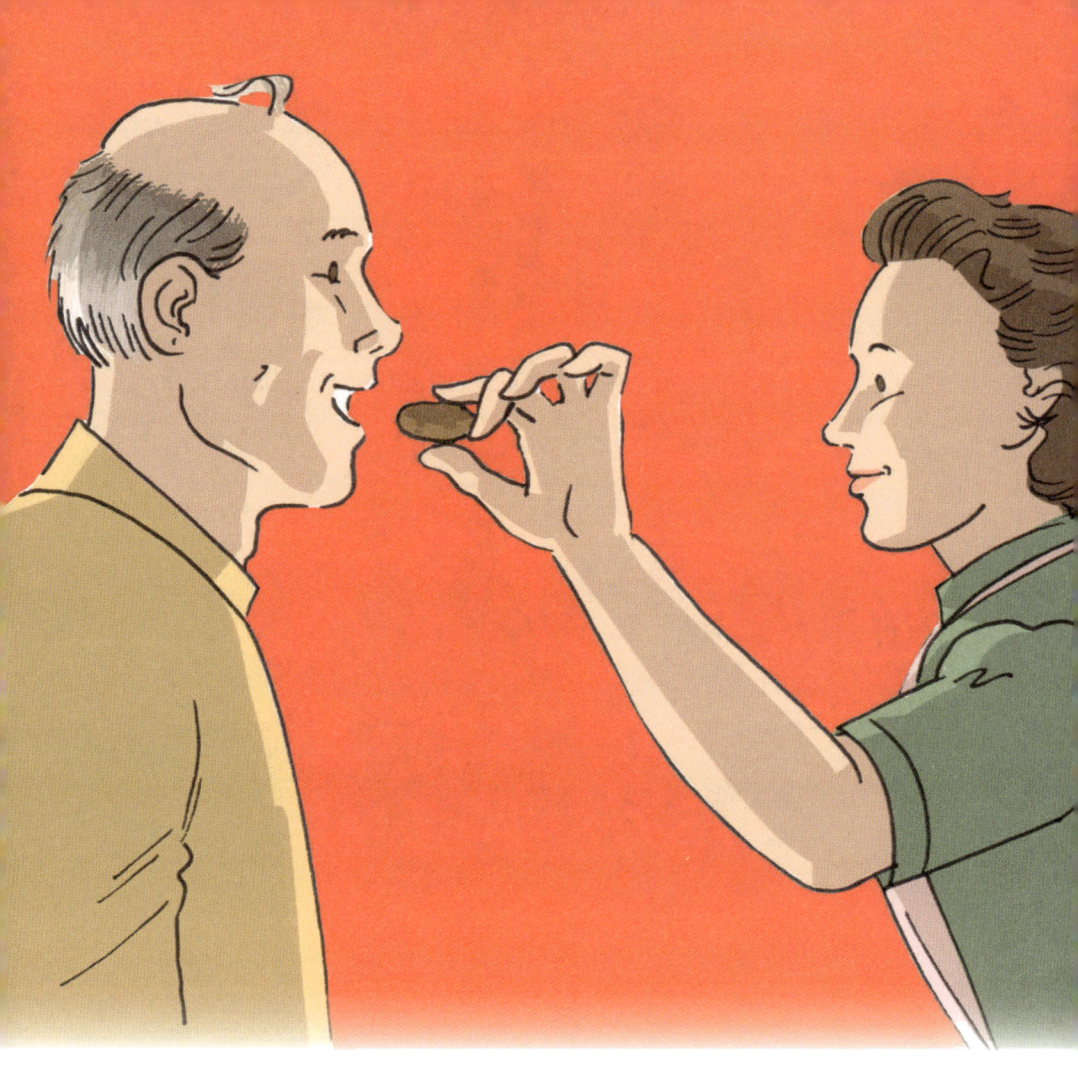

"I am happy to test anything you cook," Kenneth would say. Kenneth believed in Ruth. He also loved eating yummy food.

One night Ruth couldn't sleep.

Her tummy rumbled.

"I need a snack," she said.

She walked down to the kitchen.

Ruth munched on a butterscotch cookie. "I'm still hungry," she said.

Ruth opened the cupboard.

She got out a chocolate bar.

She took a bite and smiled.

"Perfect," Ruth said.

She ran back upstairs.

"I have an idea!" she said.

Kenneth just snored.

The next day Ruth put on her apron. She got out the ingredients for her butterscotch cookies.

"I need butter, sugar, eggs, and flour," Ruth said to herself.

"But today I also want to add something special."

Ruth got some more Nestlé chocolate out of the cupboard.

Ruth cut the chocolate into pieces.

She added it to her cookie dough.

"Here we go," she said.

Ruth put the cookies into the oven.

The first batch took about

ten minutes to bake.

But to Ruth, it felt like an hour.

Finally her cookies were done.

Kenneth walked into the kitchen.

"Something smells great!" he said.

"Let's give them a try," Ruth said.

"Yum!" said Kenneth.

"Yum!" said Ruth.

The cookies were delicious.

Ruth started serving the new cookies at her restaurant. They came with a dish of ice cream.

"What are these magical cookies?" people asked.

"I call them chocolate crunch cookies," Ruth said.

Everyone wanted Ruth's recipe.
And she was happy to share it so
that people could bake
their own cookies at home.

People even sent the cookies to soldiers fighting in the Second World War. Soon every soldier was asking for some of Ruth's cookies!

The boss at Nestlé had an idea. "Can we print your recipe on our chocolate bars?" he asked.

The boss knew Nestlé should pay Ruth for her recipe.

"We will give you a lifetime supply of chocolate," he said.

Ruth's eyes lit up.

"It's a deal," she said.

There would be no chocolate chip cookie without Ruth's bright idea. Ruth changed cookie history.

So think of Ruth the next time you bite into a chocolate chip cookie. She made our lives so much sweeter.

More I CAN READ! books for you to love:

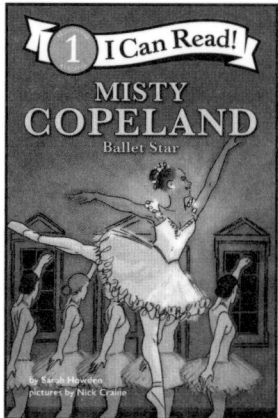

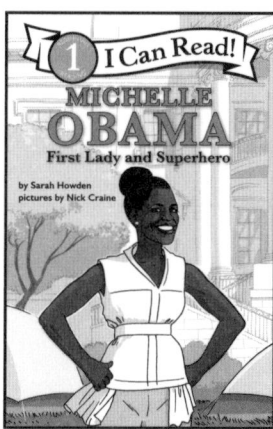

Visit **www.icanread.ca** for
a complete list of **I Can Read** books,
as well as tips for parents and educators!

1 I Can Read

BEGINNING READING

Where would we be without Ruth Graves Wakefield? Well, we wouldn't have any chocolate chip cookies! Ruth's cookies became so famous that she traded her recipe for a lifetime supply of chocolate!

My First — Ideal for sharing with emergent readers

1 — Short sentences, familiar words, and simple concepts for children eager to read on their own

2 — Engaging stories for developing readers

3 — Complex plots for confident readers

GUIDED READING LEVEL J

Collins
An Imprint of HarperCollinsPublishers
www.icanread.ca

Cover art © 2019 by Nick Craine

An **I Can Read** Book

www.harpercollins.ca
CAN $5.99 / ISBN 978-1-4434-5986-0